Saturn

by Derek Zobel

Consultant:
Duane Quam, M.S. Physics
Chair, Minnesota State
Academic Science Standards
Writing Committee

BELLWETHER MEDIA · MINNEAPOLIS, MN

Note to Librarians, Teachers, and Parents:

Blastoff! Readers are carefully developed by literacy experts and combine standards-based content with developmentally appropriate text.

Level 1 provides the most support through repetition of high-frequency words, light text, predictable sentence patterns, and strong visual support.

Level 2 offers early readers a bit more challenge through varied simple sentences, increased text load, and less repetition of high-frequency words.

Level 3 advances early-fluent readers toward fluency through increased text and concept load, less reliance on visuals, longer sentences, and more literary language.

Level 4 builds reading stamina by providing more text per page, increased use of punctuation, greater variation in sentence patterns, and increasingly challenging vocabulary.

Level 5 encourages children to move from "learning to read" to "reading to learn" by providing even more text, varied writing styles, and less familiar topics.

Whichever book is right for your reader, Blastoff! Readers are the perfect books to build confidence and encourage a love of reading that will last a lifetime!

This edition first published in 2010 by Bellwether Media, Inc.

No part of this publication may be reproduced in whole or in part without written permission of the publisher. For information regarding permission, write to Bellwether Media, Inc., Attention: Permissions Department, 5357 Penn Avenue South, Minneapolis, MN 55419.

Library of Congress Cataloging-in-Publication Data

Zobel, Derek, 1983-
  Saturn / by Derek Zobel.
    p. cm. – (Blastoff! readers. exploring space)
  Includes bibliographical references and index.
  Summary: "Introductory text and full-color images explore the physical characteristics and discovery of the planet Saturn. Intended for students in kindergarten through third grade"–Provided by publisher.
  ISBN 978-1-60014-407-3 (hardcover : alk. paper)
  1. Saturn (Planet)–Juvenile literature. I. Title.
  QB671.Z63 2010
  523.46–dc22   2009038274

010110   1149

Contents

What Is Saturn?   4

Saturn and the Sun   6

Rings and Moons   14

Exploring Saturn   17

Glossary   22

To Learn More   23

Index   24

Saturn is a **planet**.
It is a **gas giant**.
It is named after the
Roman god
of farming.

rings

Saturn can be seen from Earth without a telescope. It has the largest **rings** of any planet.

Saturn

Saturn is the sixth planet from the sun. All of the planets **orbit** the sun.

6

Saturn's orbit is oval-shaped. The planet can be as close as 840 million miles (1.4 billion kilometers) or as far as 940 million miles (1.5 billion kilometers) from the sun.

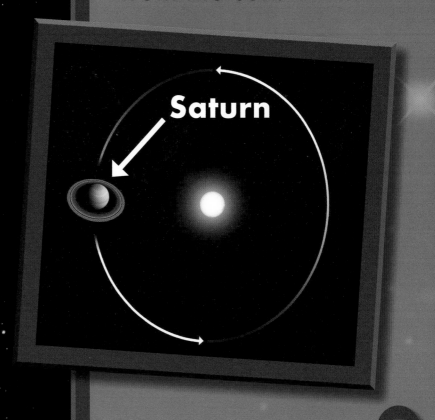

Saturn

Earth orbits the sun once in 365 days, or one year. Saturn takes 10,759 Earth days to orbit the sun once. A Saturn year takes almost 30 Earth years!

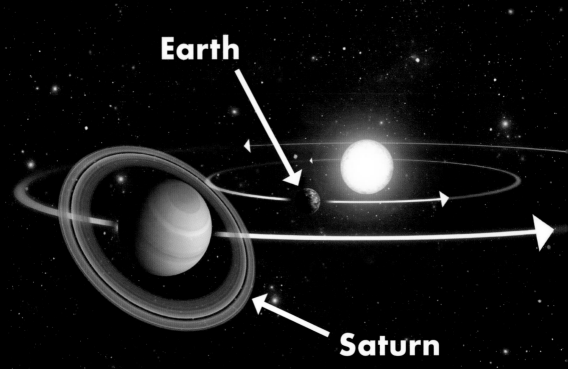

Earth

Saturn

axis

All of the planets spin on their **axis** as they orbit the sun. A complete spin is called a day.

Earth takes 24 hours to spin on its axis one time. Saturn completes one spin in 11 Earth hours.

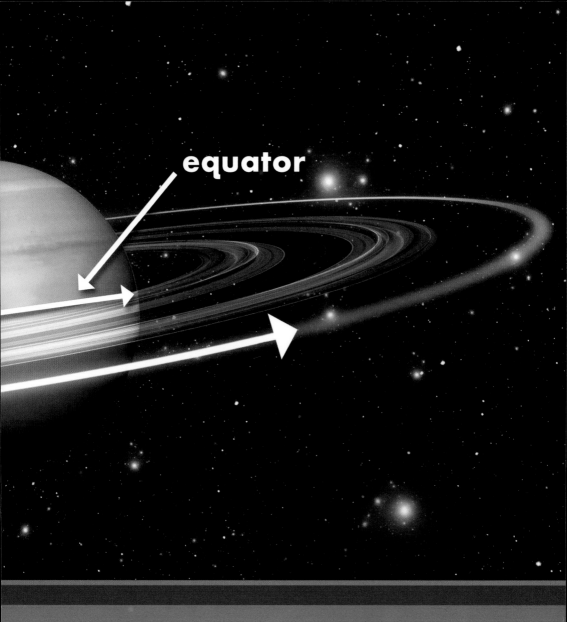

equator

It spins at 22,000 miles (35,500 kilometers) per hour. That is fast enough to make Saturn bulge at its **equator**.

Saturn is the second biggest planet in the **solar system**. About 763 Earths could fit inside Saturn!

Earth

Saturn

Saturn is 74,900 miles (120,540 kilometers) across at its equator. It is thinner from **pole** to pole.

Saturn has seven rings. The rings are made mainly of ice. They surround Saturn at its equator.

The rings are very thin.
They range in thickness
from 660 to 9,800 feet
(200 to 3,000 meters).

Titan

Saturn has 25 **moons** that measure more than 6 miles (10 kilometers) across. The largest moon is Titan. It is larger than the planet Mercury!

Many **space probes** have explored and taken photographs of Saturn.

Pioneer-Saturn flew by Saturn in 1979. It discovered two of Saturn's rings.

Pioneer-Saturn

Voyager 1

Voyager 1 and *Voyager 2* passed by Saturn in the early 1980s. They found that Saturn's rings were made of **ringlets**.

In 2004, *Cassini-Huygens* began orbiting Saturn.

Cassini-Huygens

Cassini-Huygens is studying Saturn and its moon Titan. It sends new information back to Earth every day!

Glossary

axis—an imaginary line that runs through the center of a planet; a planet spins on its axis.

equator—an imaginary line that circles a planet around its width

gas giant—a planet made up mainly of gas instead of rock

moons—space objects that orbit a planet or other space object

orbit—to travel around the sun or other object in space

planet—a large, round space object that orbits the sun and is alone in its orbit

pole—the point at the top and bottom of a planet

ringlets—thin rings that make up the larger rings of Saturn

rings—flat bands made of pieces of rock, dust, and ice that form around a planet; rings look solid from far away.

Roman god—a god worshipped by the people of ancient Rome; Saturn was the god of farming.

solar system—the sun and the objects that orbit it; the solar system has planets, moons, comets, and asteroids.

space probes—spacecraft that explore planets and other space objects and send information back to Earth; space probes do not carry people.

To Learn More

AT THE LIBRARY

Bortolotti, Dan. *Exploring Saturn*. Toronto, Ont.: Firefly Books, 2003.

McGranaghan, John. *Saturn for My Birthday*. Mt. Pleasant, S.C.: Sylvan Dell Publishing, 2008.

Taylor-Butler, Christine. *Saturn*. New York, N.Y.: Children's Press, 2008.

ON THE WEB

Learning more about Saturn is as easy as 1, 2, 3.

1. Go to www.factsurfer.com.

2. Enter "Saturn" into the search box.

3. Click the "Surf" button and you will see a list of related Web sites.

With factsurfer.com, finding more information is just a click away.

BLASTOFF! JIMMY CHALLENGE

Blastoff! Jimmy is hidden somewhere in this book. Can you find him? If you need help, you can find a hint at the bottom of page 24.

Index

1979, 18
1980s, 19
2004, 20
axis, 9, 10
Cassini-Huygens, 20, 21
day, 8, 9, 21
Earth, 5, 8, 10, 12
equator, 11, 13, 14
gas giant, 4
Mercury, 16
moons, 16, 21
orbit, 6, 7, 8, 9, 20
Pioneer-Saturn, 18
planet, 4, 5, 6, 7, 9, 12, 16
pole, 13
ringlets, 19
rings, 5, 14, 15, 18, 19

Roman god, 4
solar system, 12
space probes, 17
sun, 6, 7, 8, 9
telescope, 5
Titan, 16, 21
Voyager 1, 19
Voyager 2, 19
year, 8

The images in this book are reproduced through the courtesy of: Mariephotos, front cover, pp. 10-11; Clara, p. 4 (small); Friedrich Saurer / Photo Researchers, Inc., pp. 4-5; NASA, pp. 6-7; Juan Eppardo, pp. 7 (small), 8-9, 9 (small); Juan Martinez, pp. 12-13; DV, p. 14 (small); Friedrich Saurer / Science Photo Library, pp. 14-15; Chris Butler / Photo Researchers, Inc., p. 16; Chad Baker, p. 17; NASA / Juan Eppardo, p. 18 (small); NASA / Mariephotos, pp. 18-19; Stocktrek Images, pp. 20-21.

Blastoff! Jimmy Challenge (from page 23).
Hint: Go to page 10 and go for a spin.